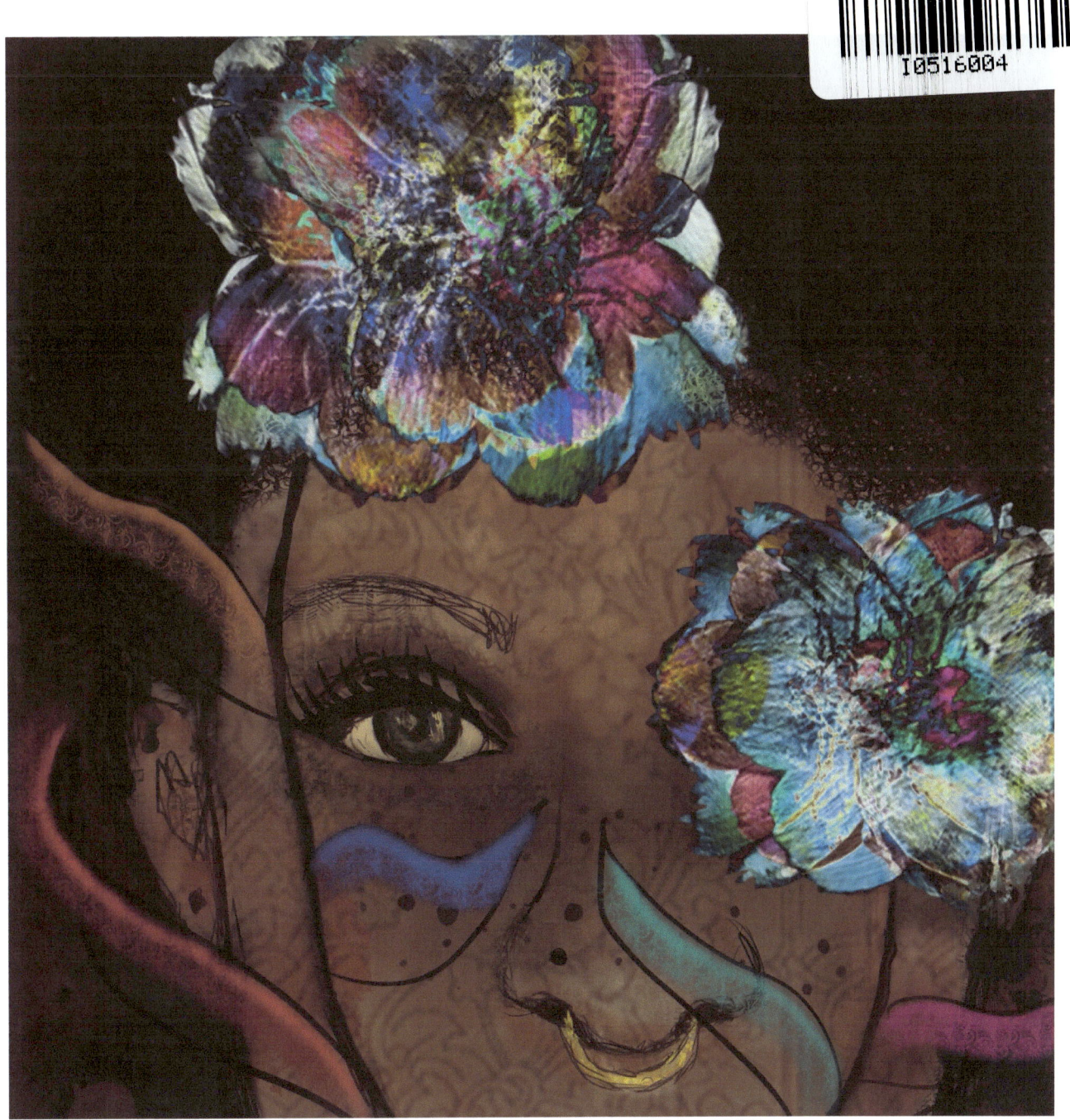

'Beneath the Color'   3000 x 3000 px

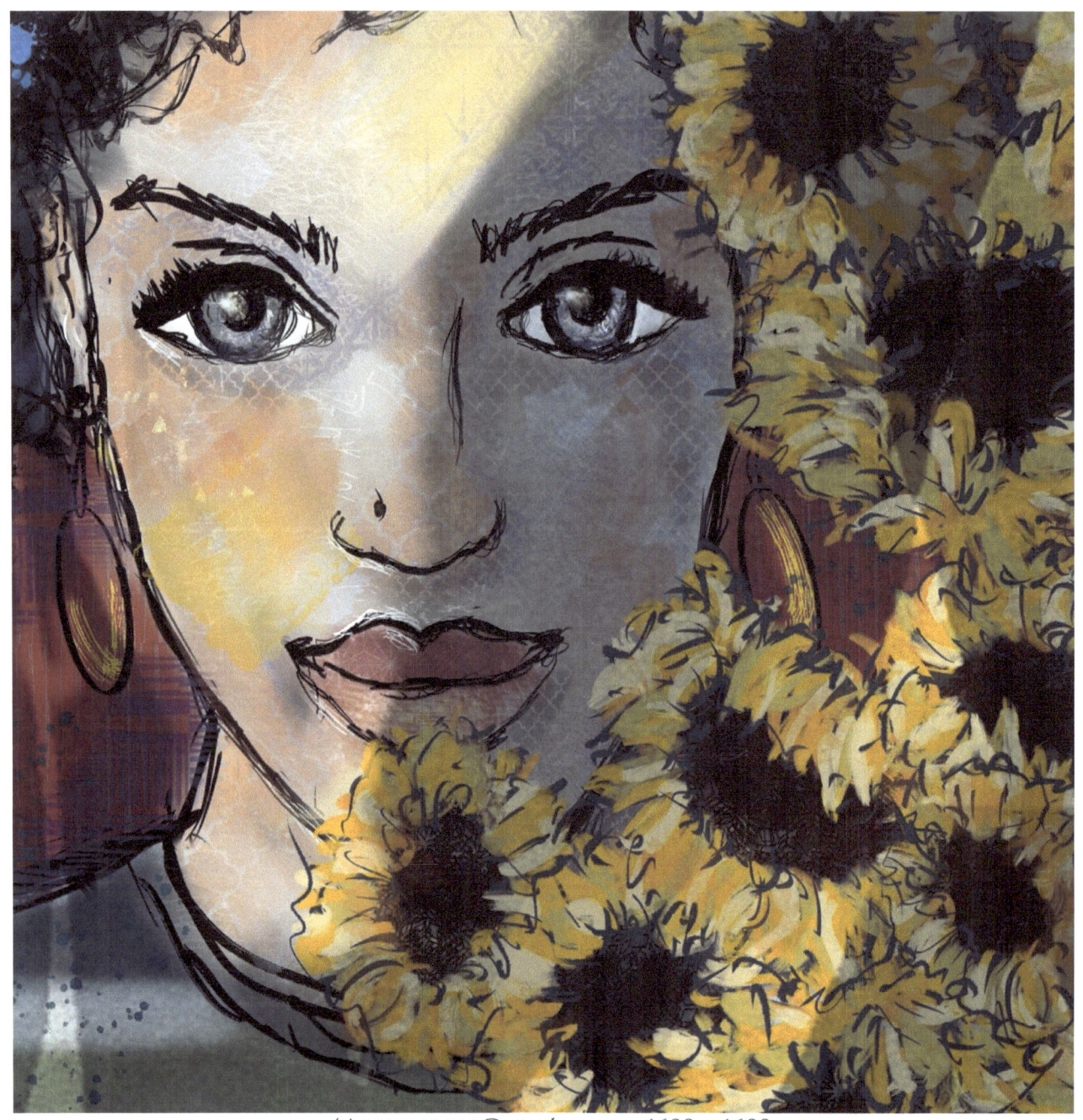

'Afternoon Glow'   4600 x 4600 px

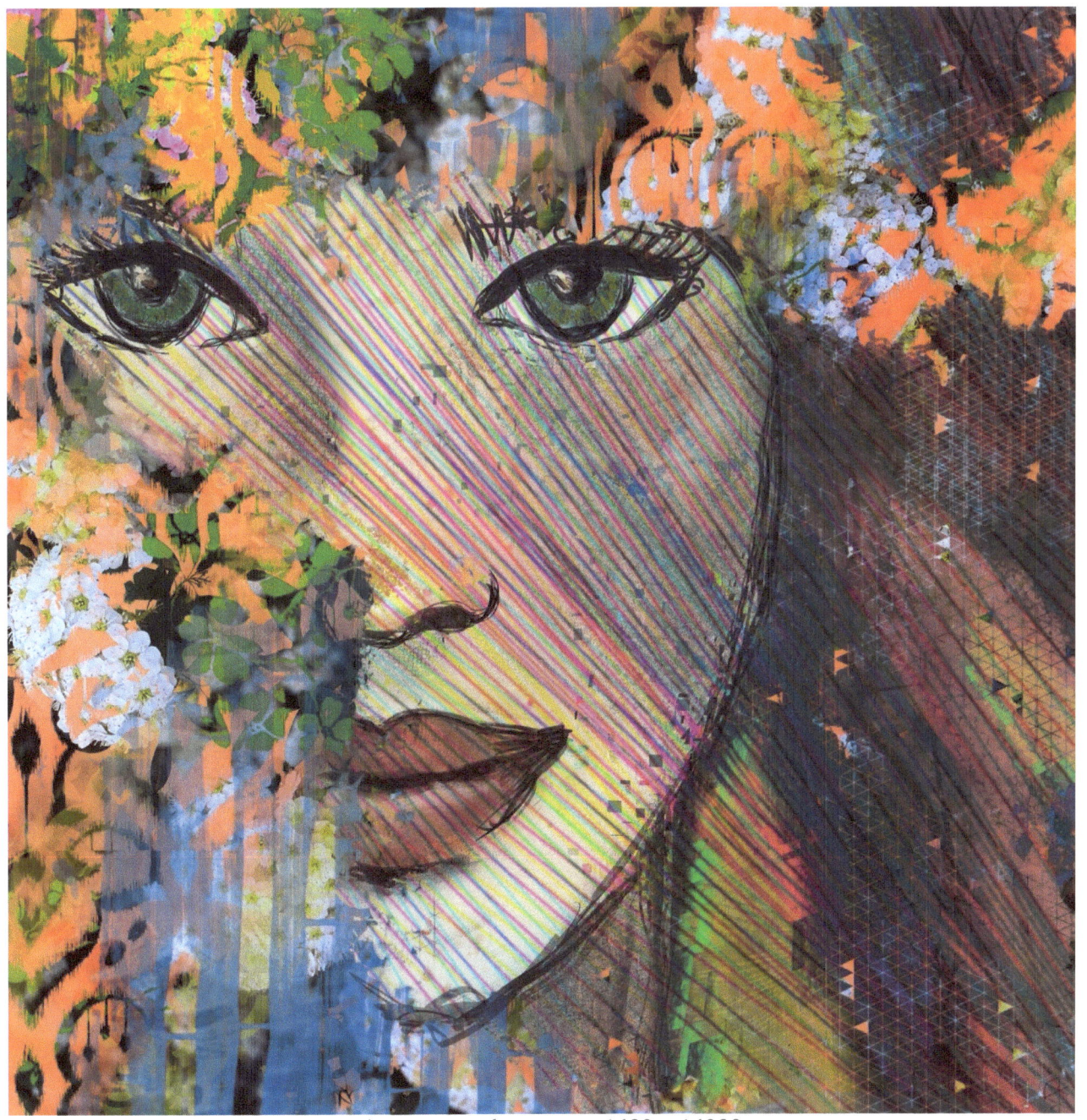

'Prismatic'   4600 x 46000 px

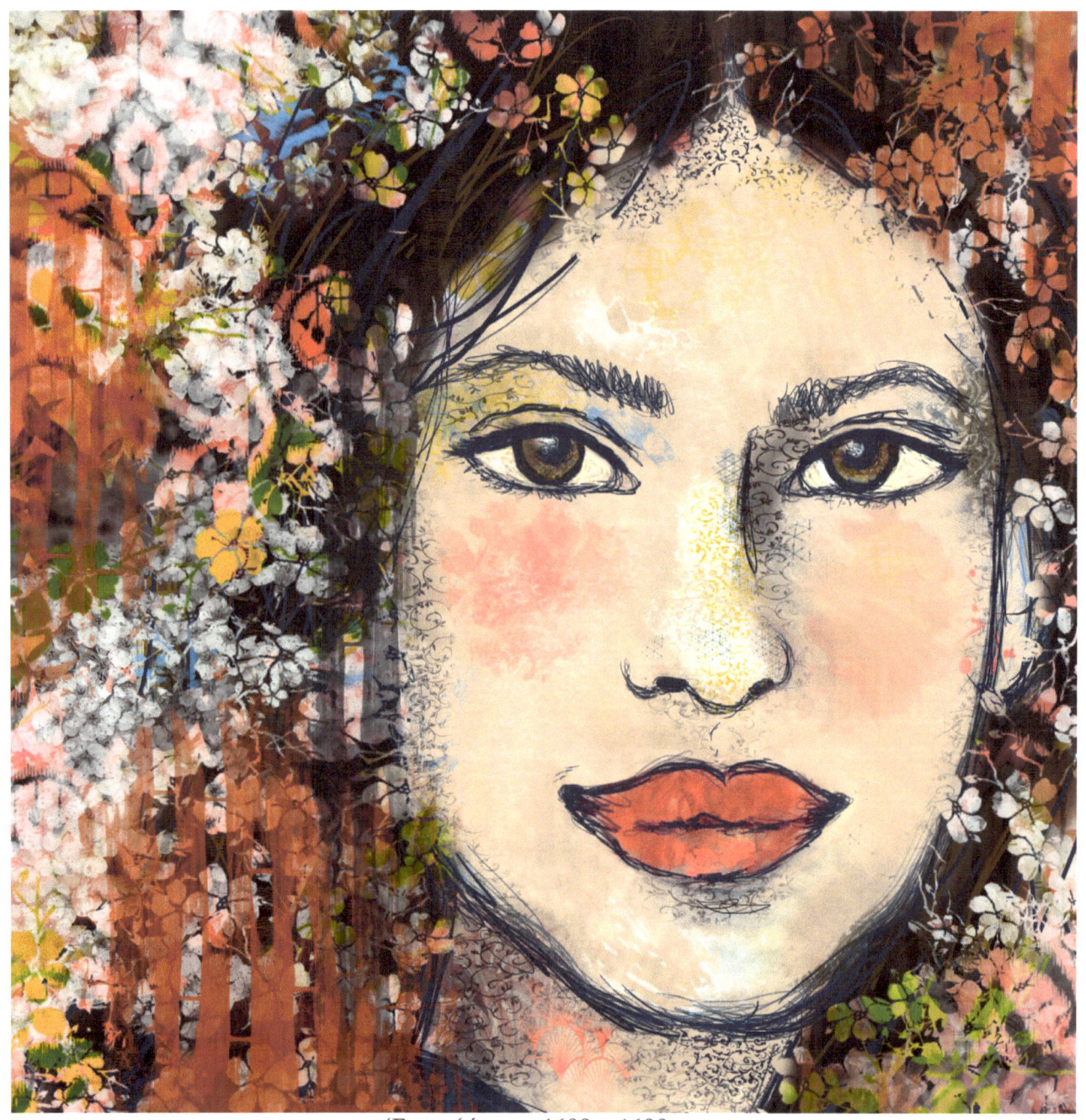

'Fierté'   4600 x 4600 px

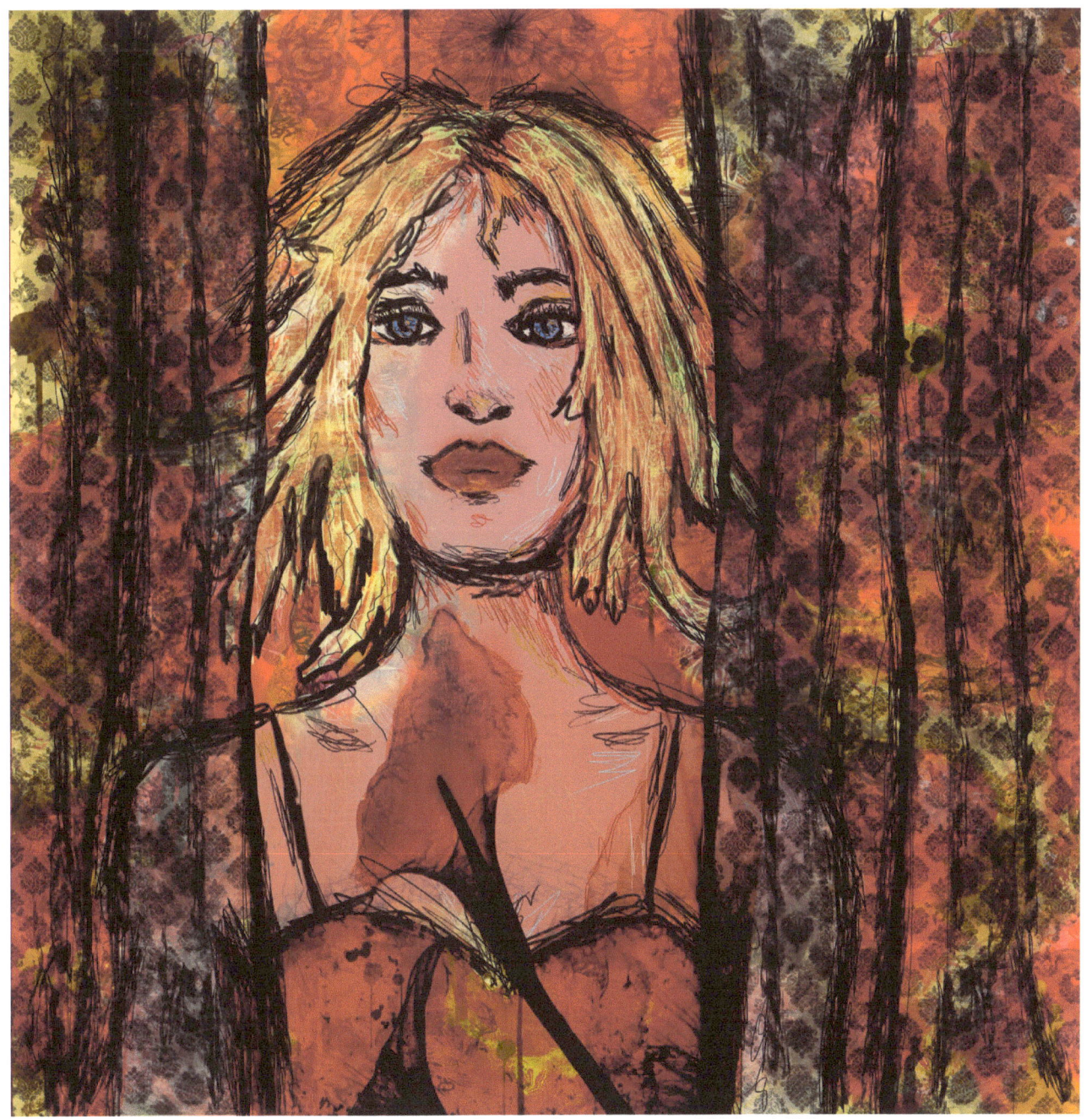

'It's Not That Simple'   4600 x 4600 px

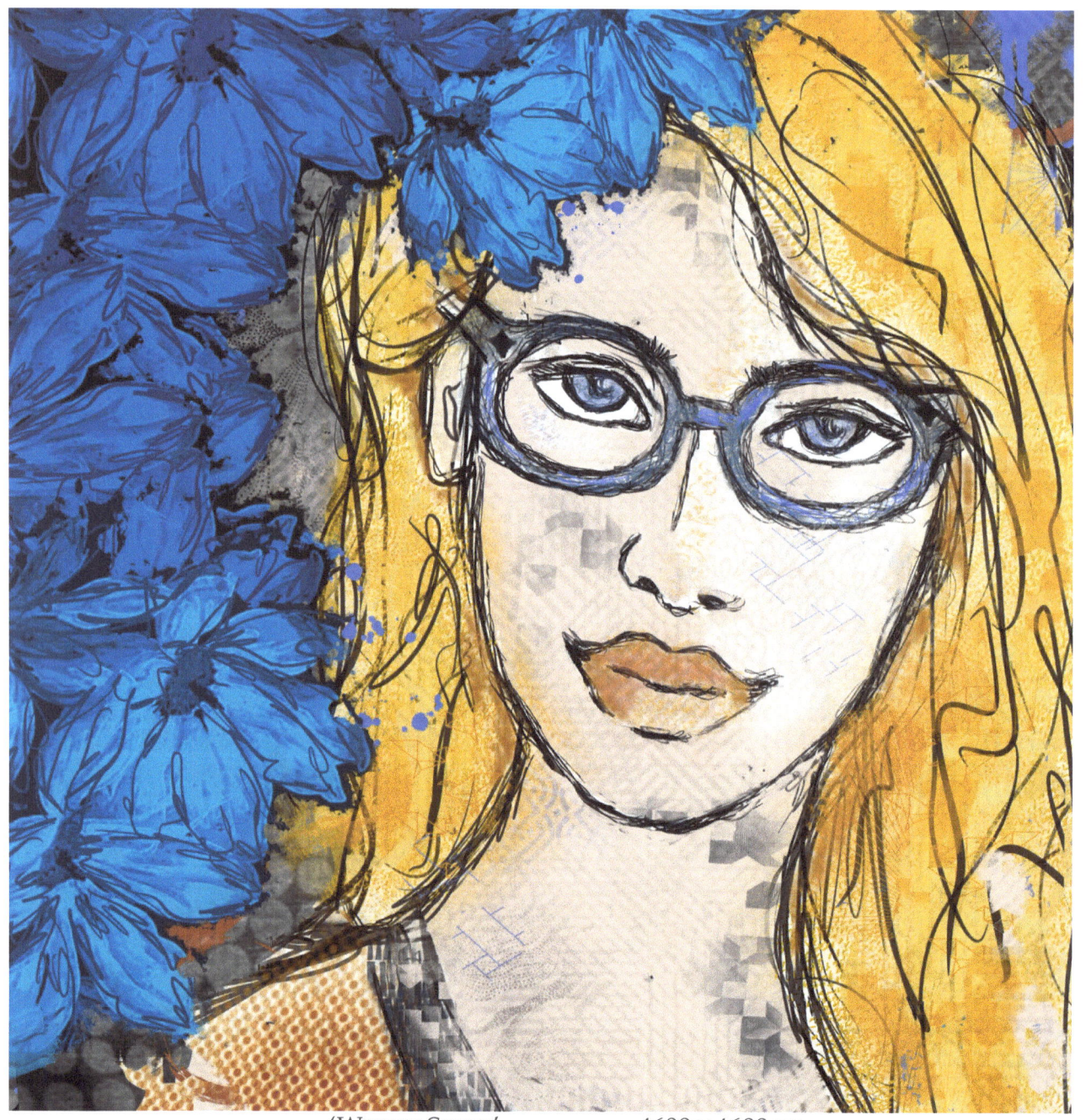

'Within Sight' 4600 x 4600 px

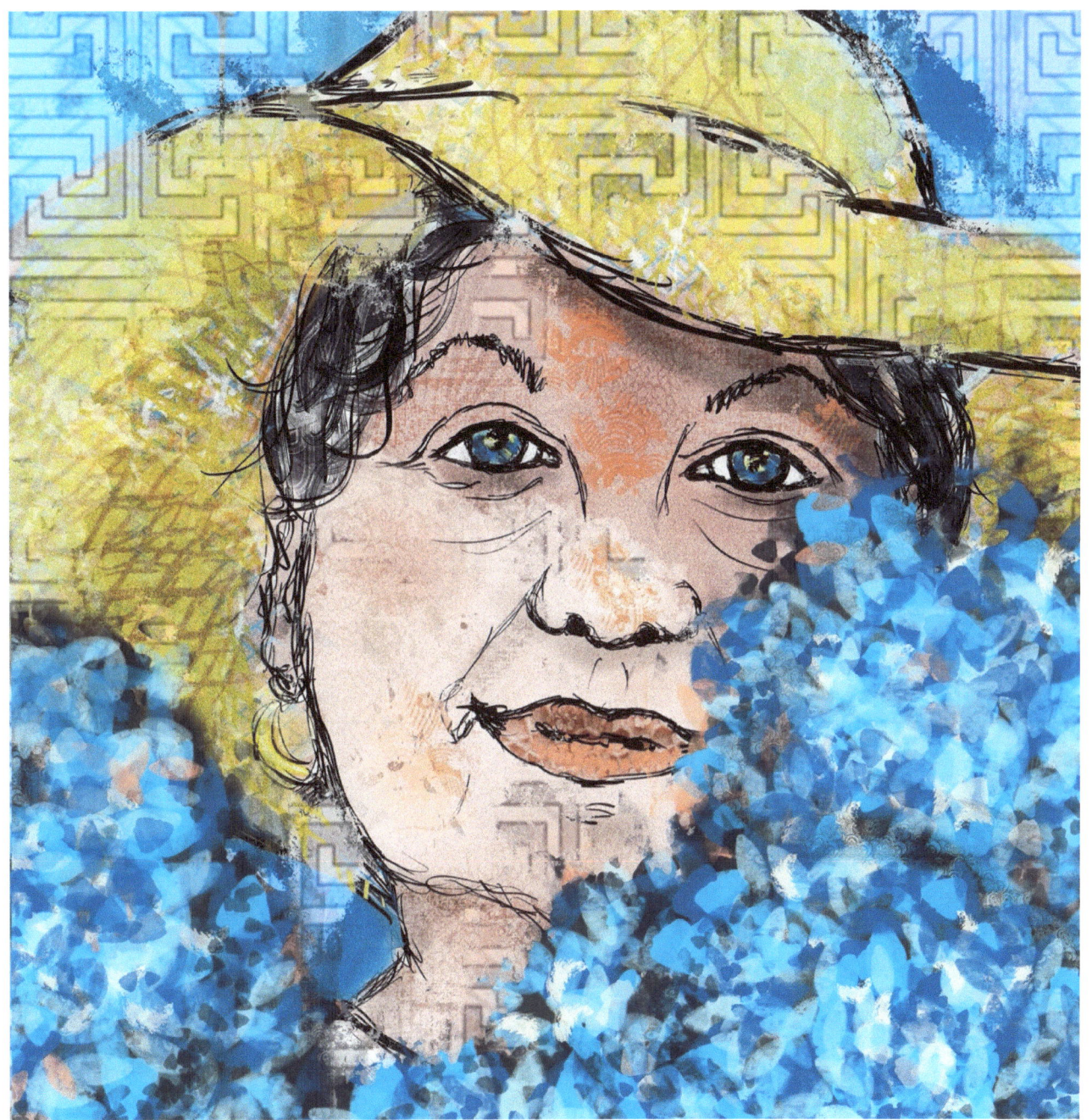

'Gracing the Beach' 4600 x 4600 px

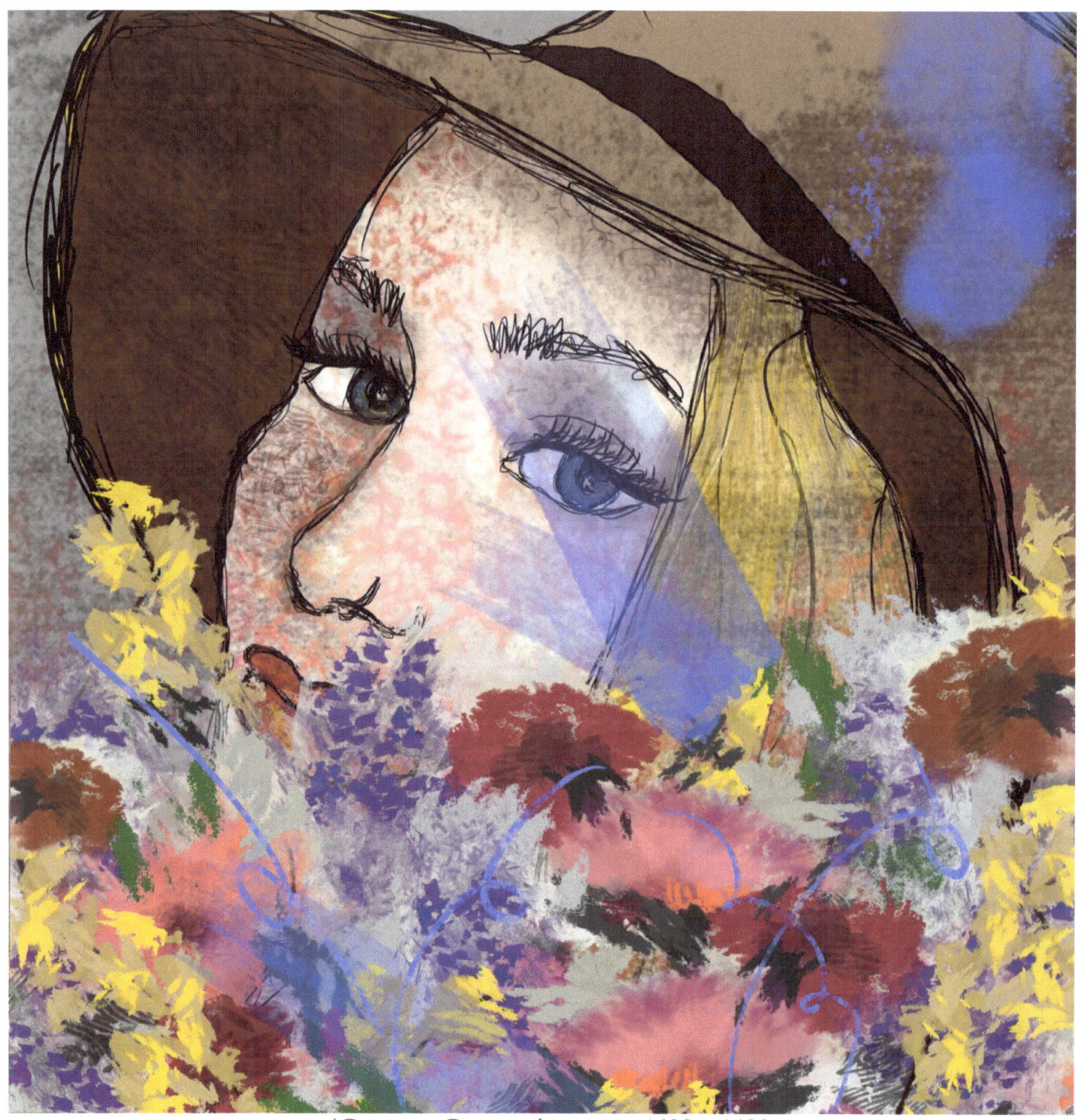

'Catch a Glimpse'   4600 x 4600 px

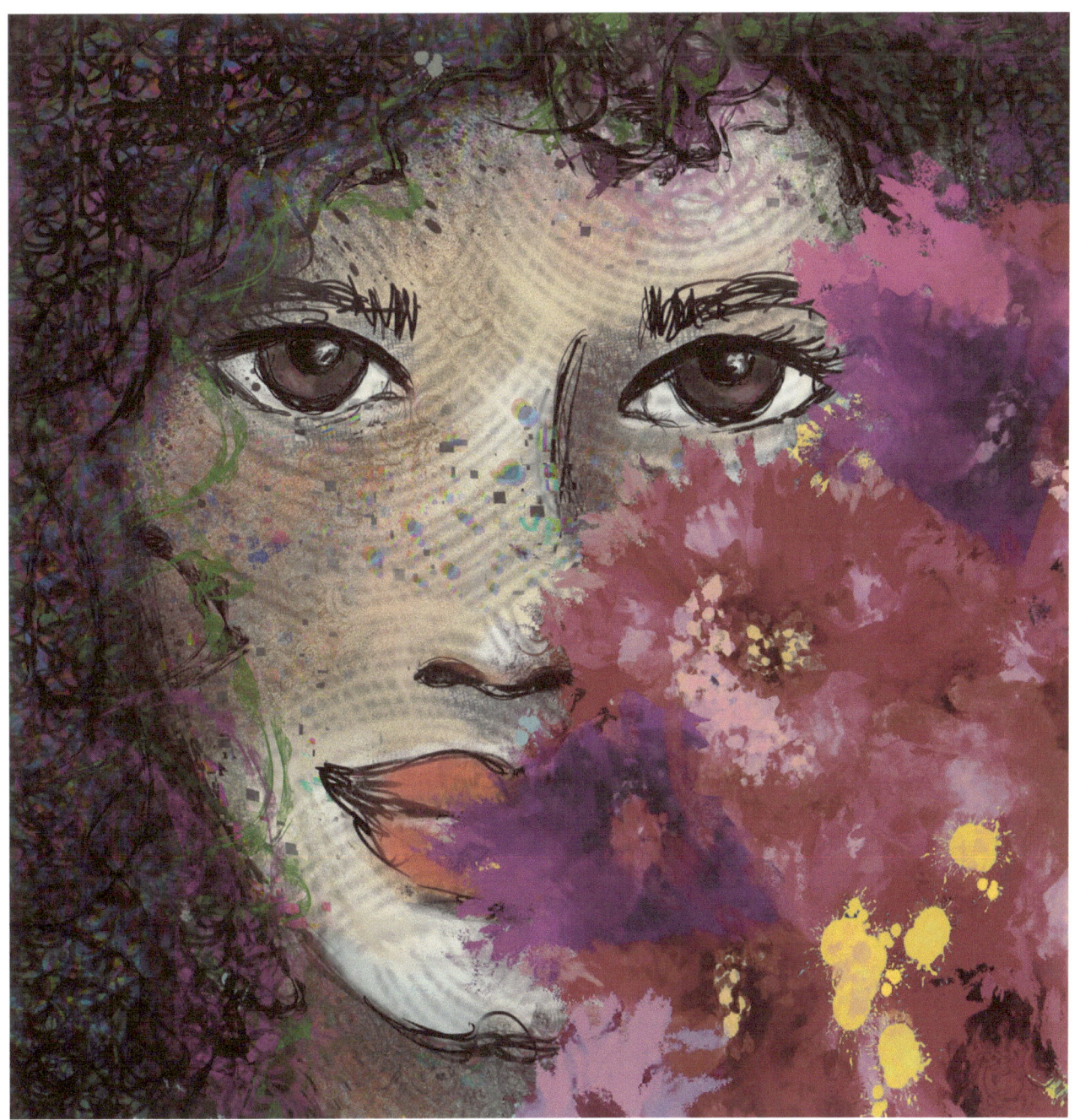

'Her Secret' 4600 x 4600 px

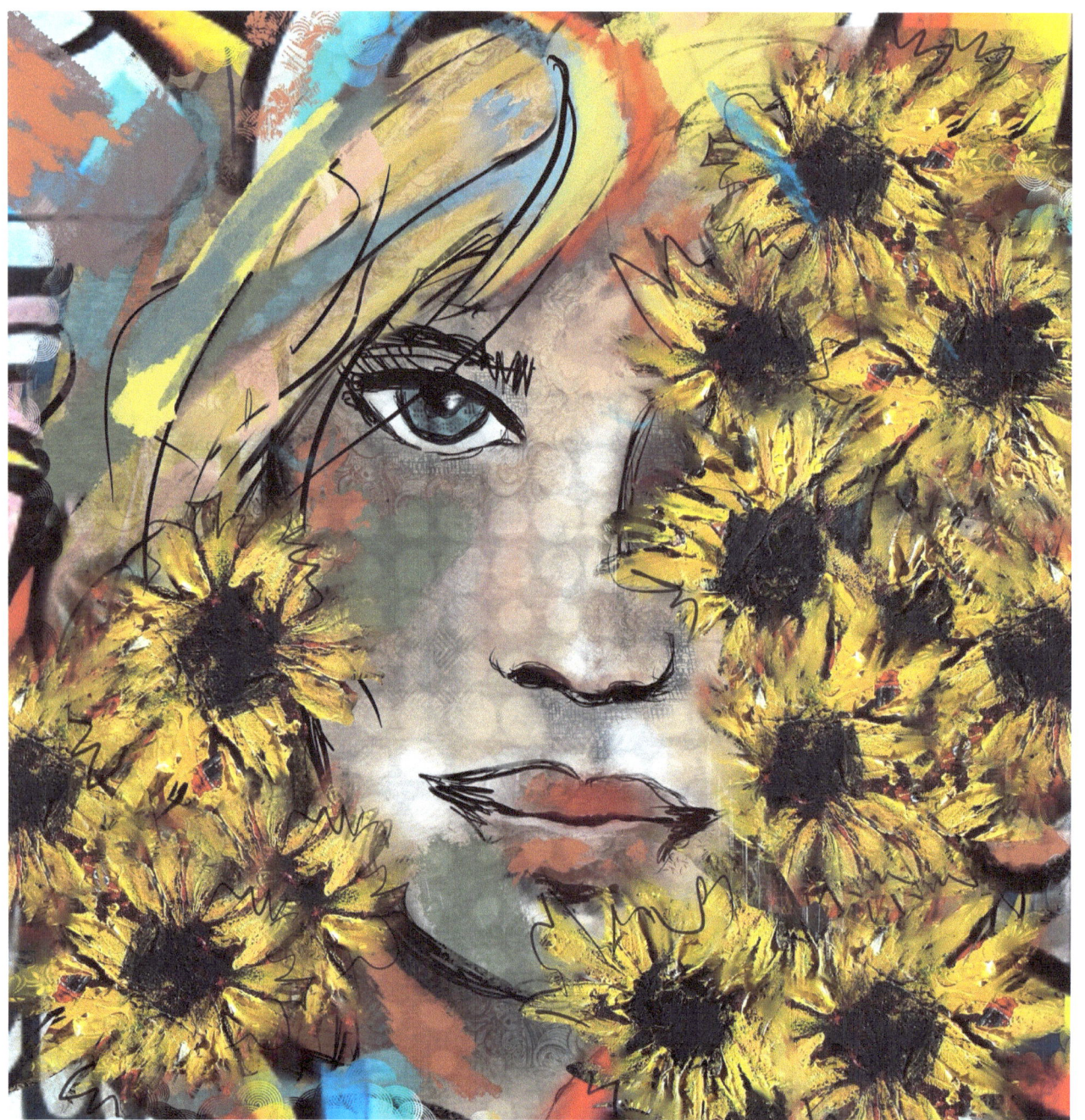

'Sheltering at Home with Sunflowers'   4600 x 4600 px

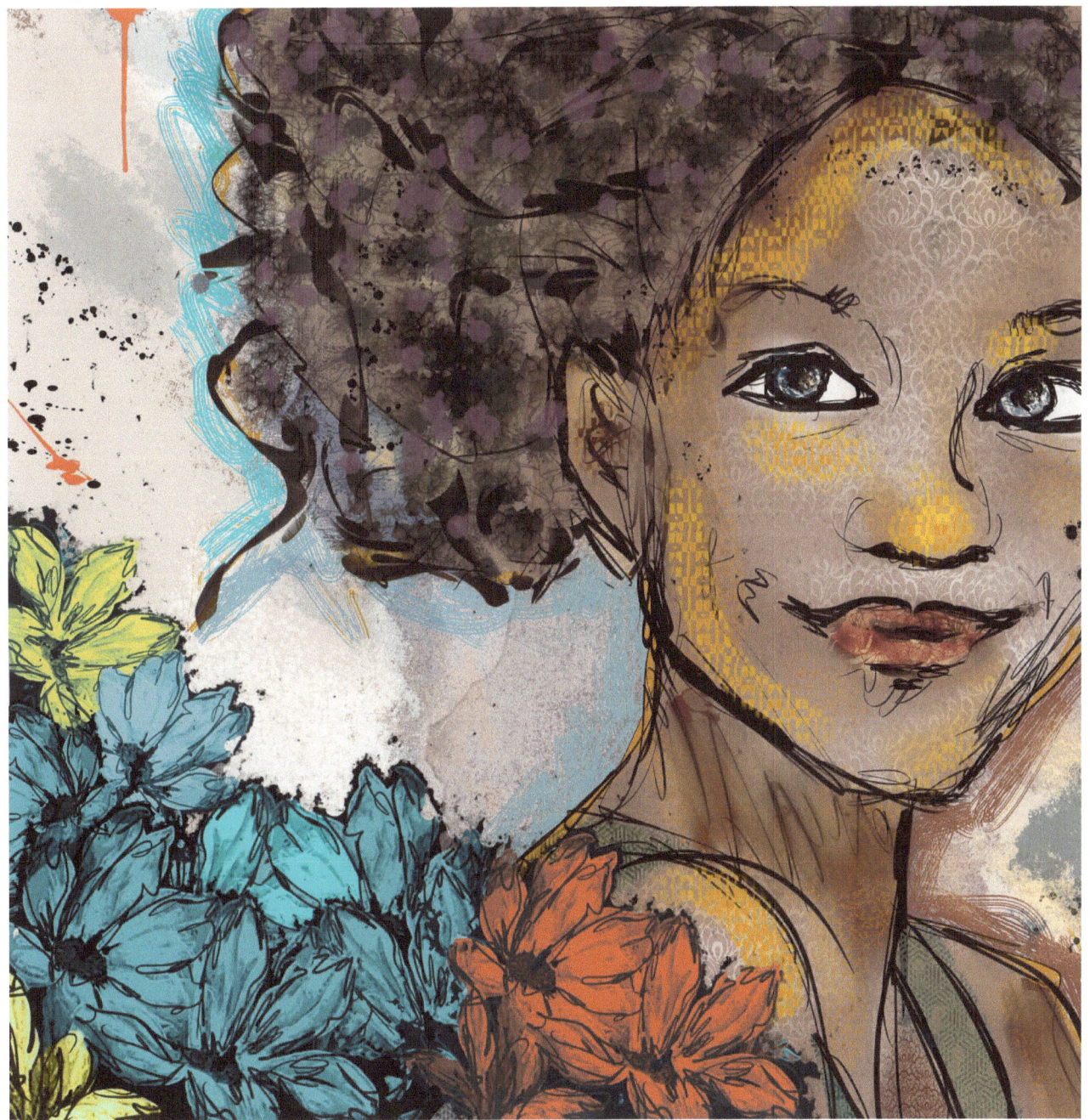

'They Should Matter' 4600 x 4600 px

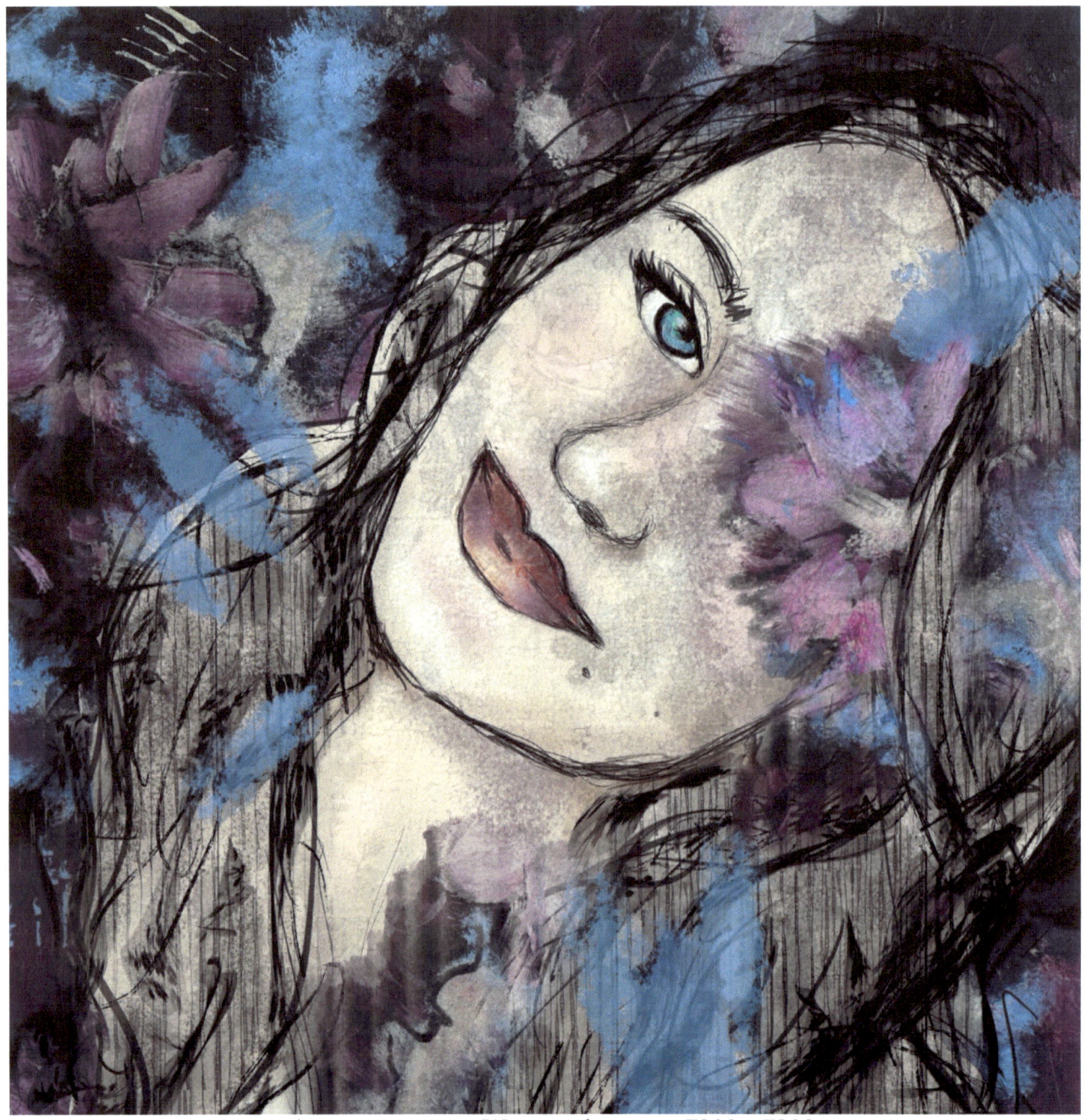

'Adventures in Wonder'   7200 x 7200 px

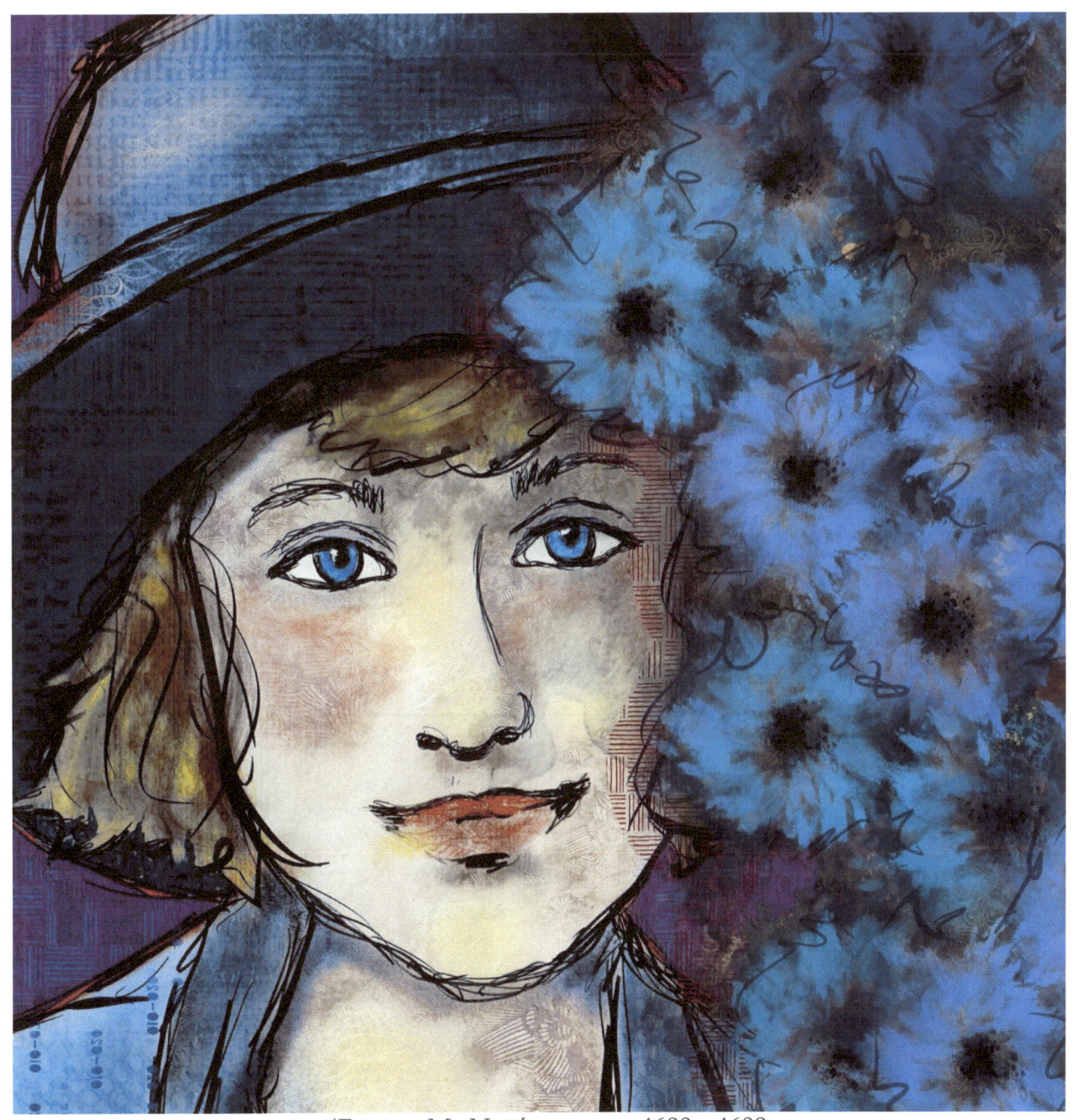

'Forget Me Not'   4600 x 4600 px

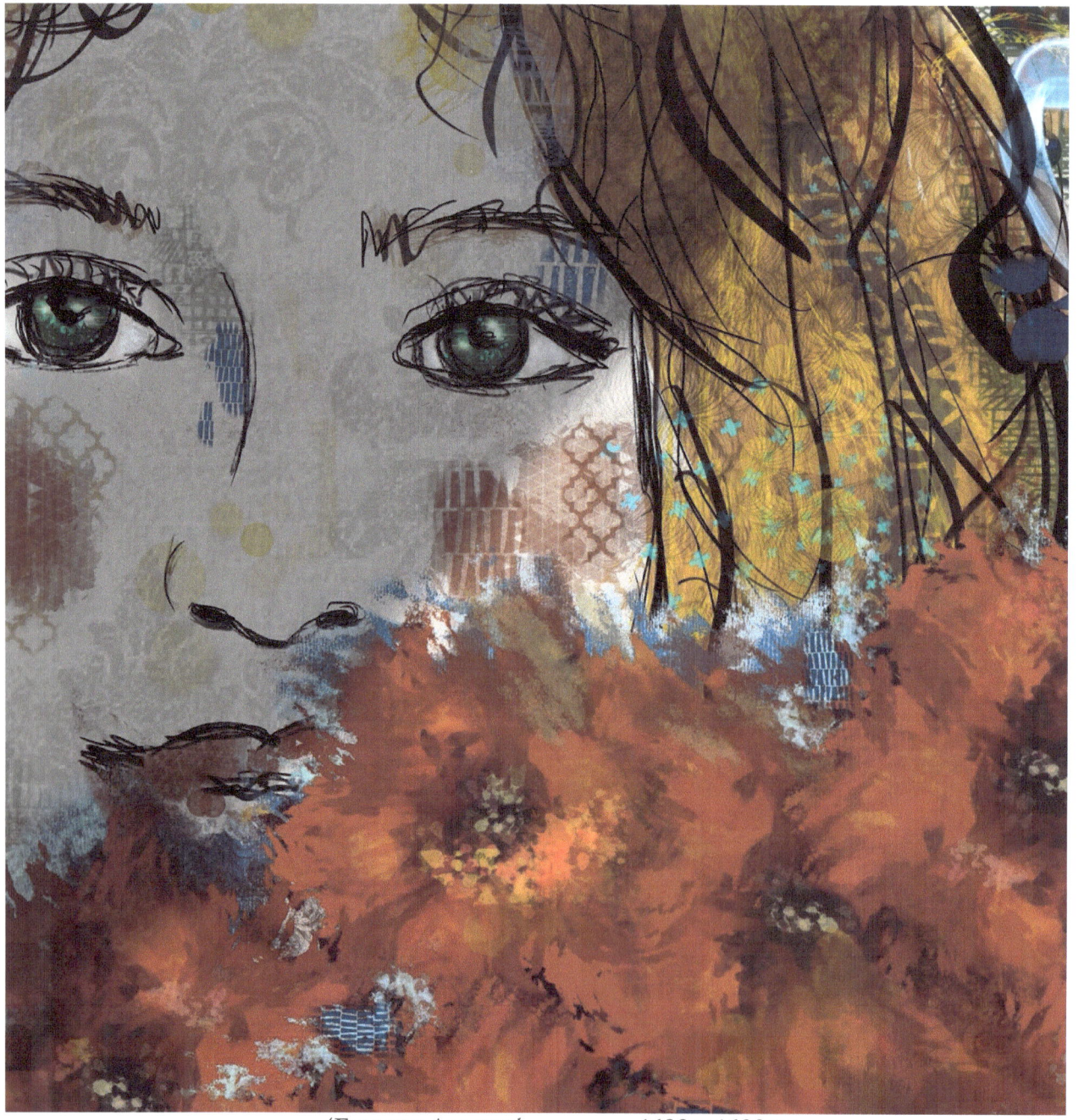

'FRENCH ALLURE'   4600 x 4600 px

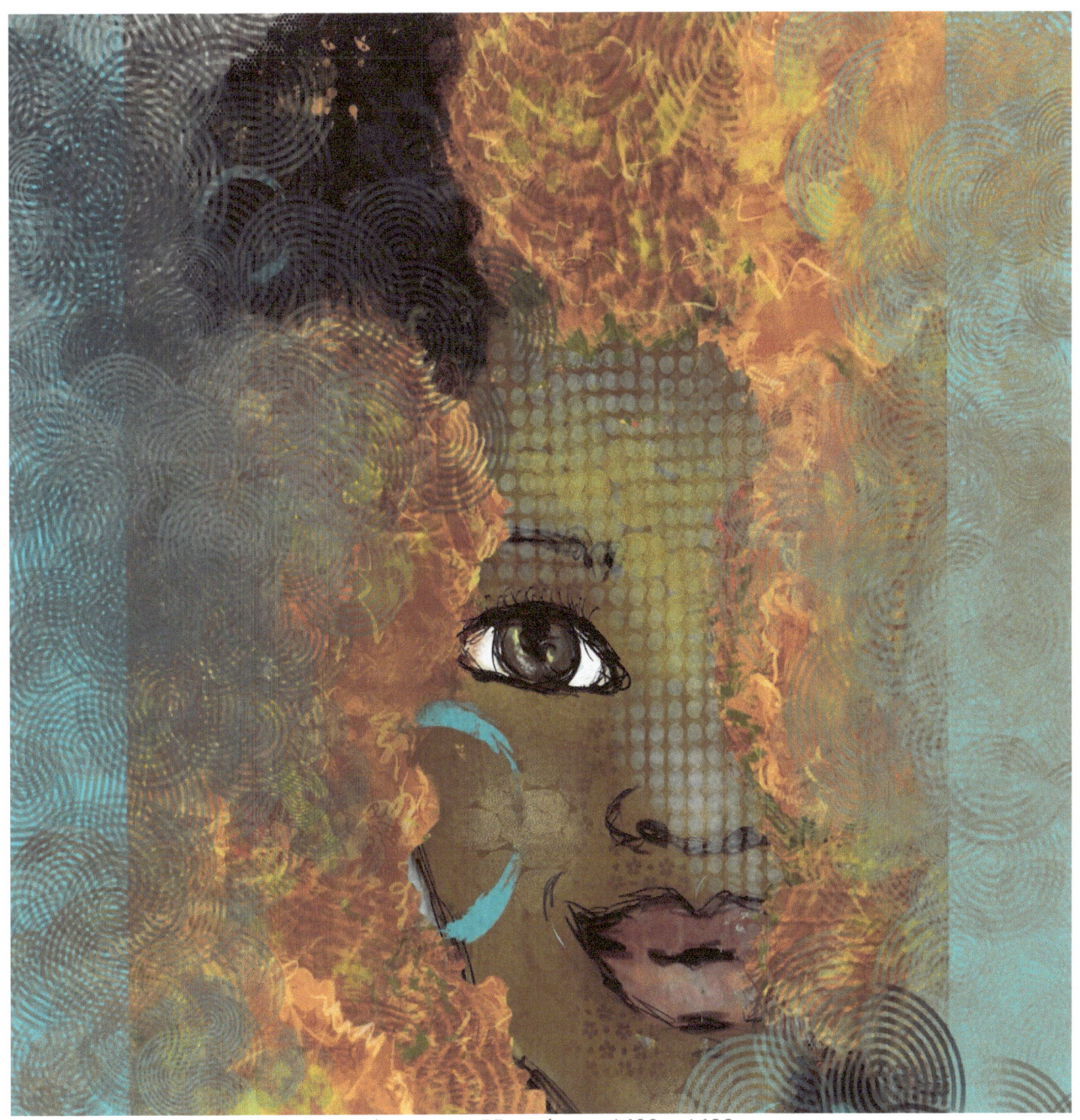

'Virtual Hugs' 4600 x 4600 px

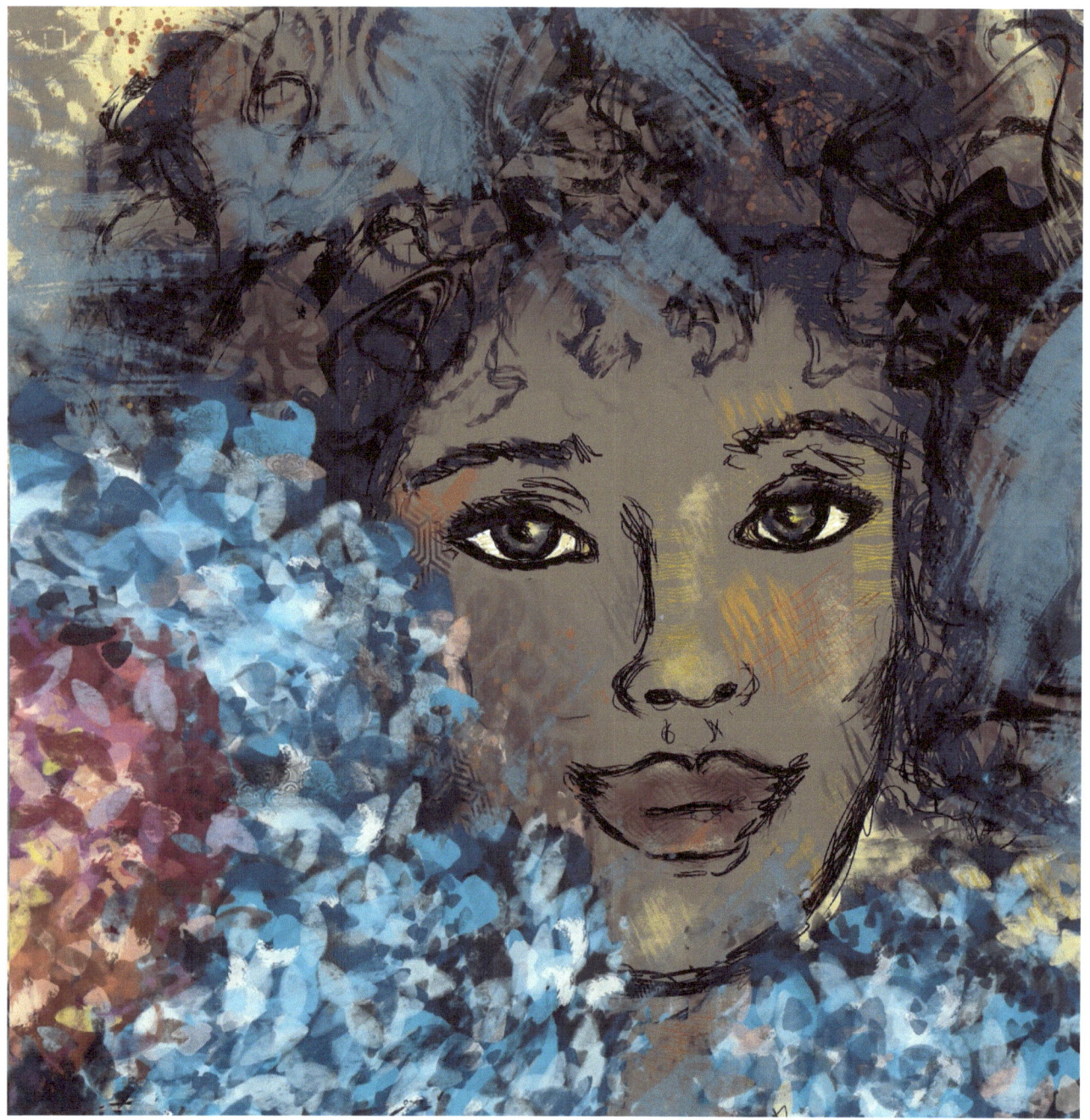

'LOVE TO CAMEROON'   4600 x 4600 px

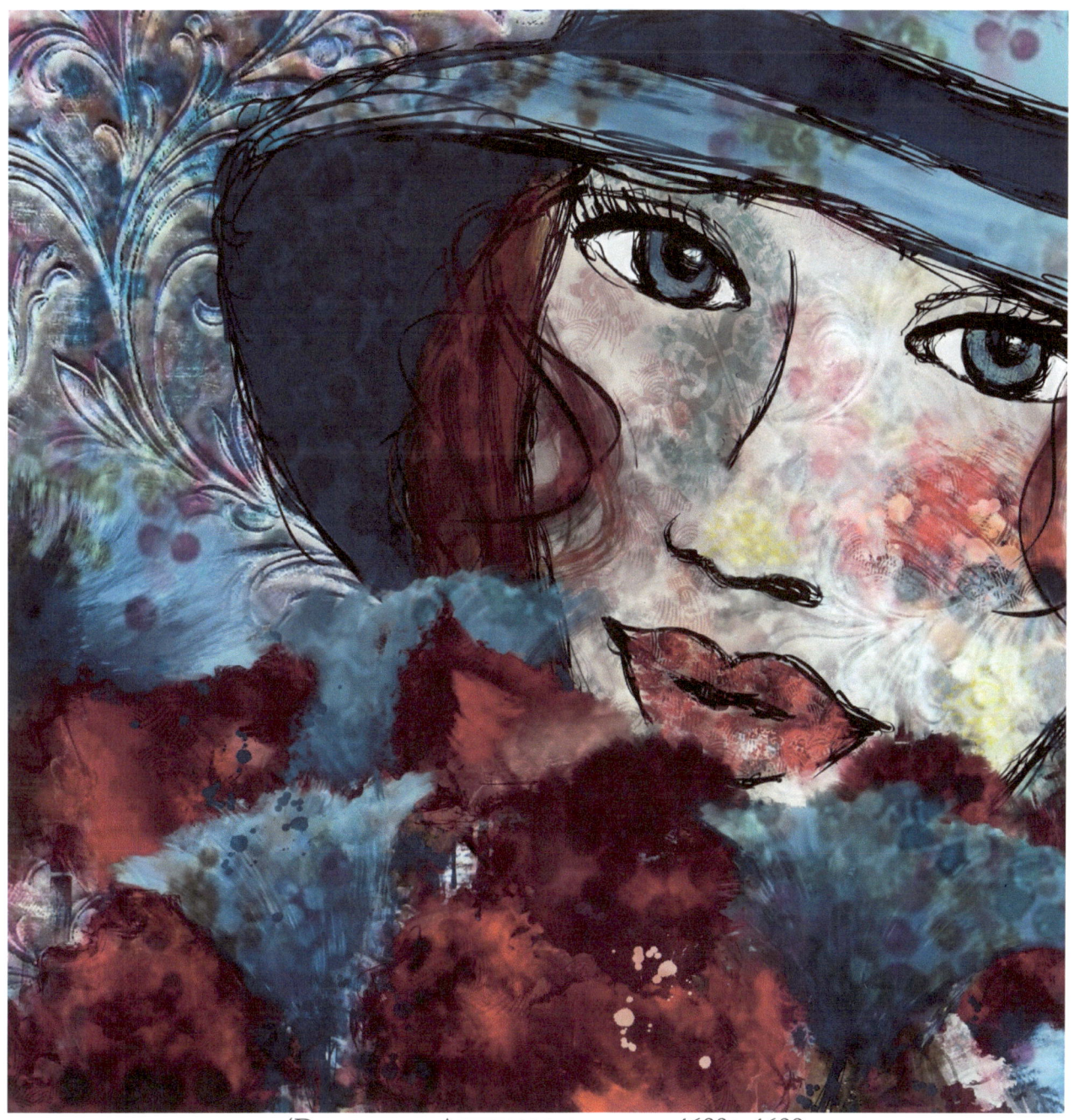

'Delightful Afternoon   4600 x 4600 px

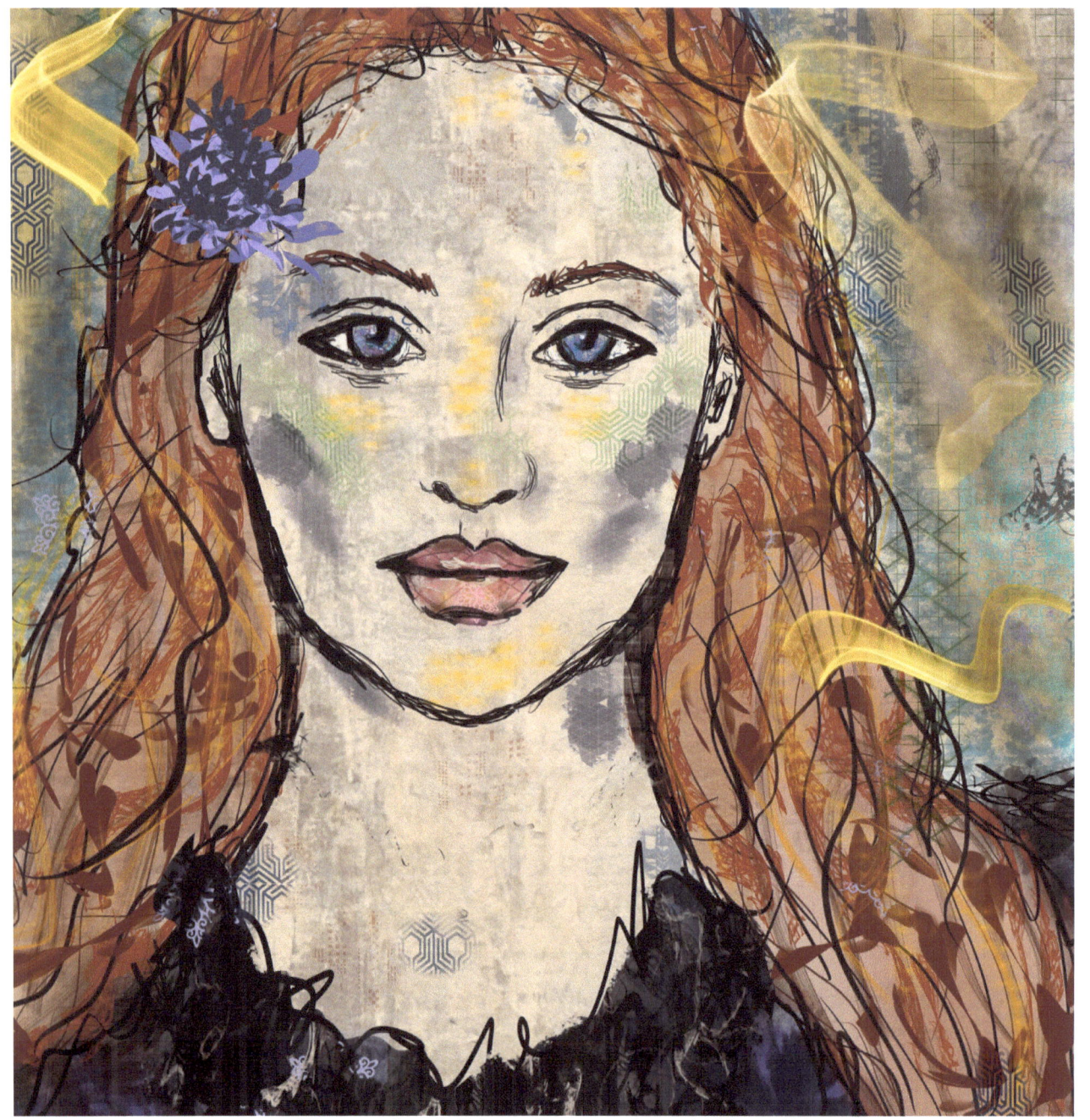

'Before Life's Many Lessons'   4600 x 4600 px

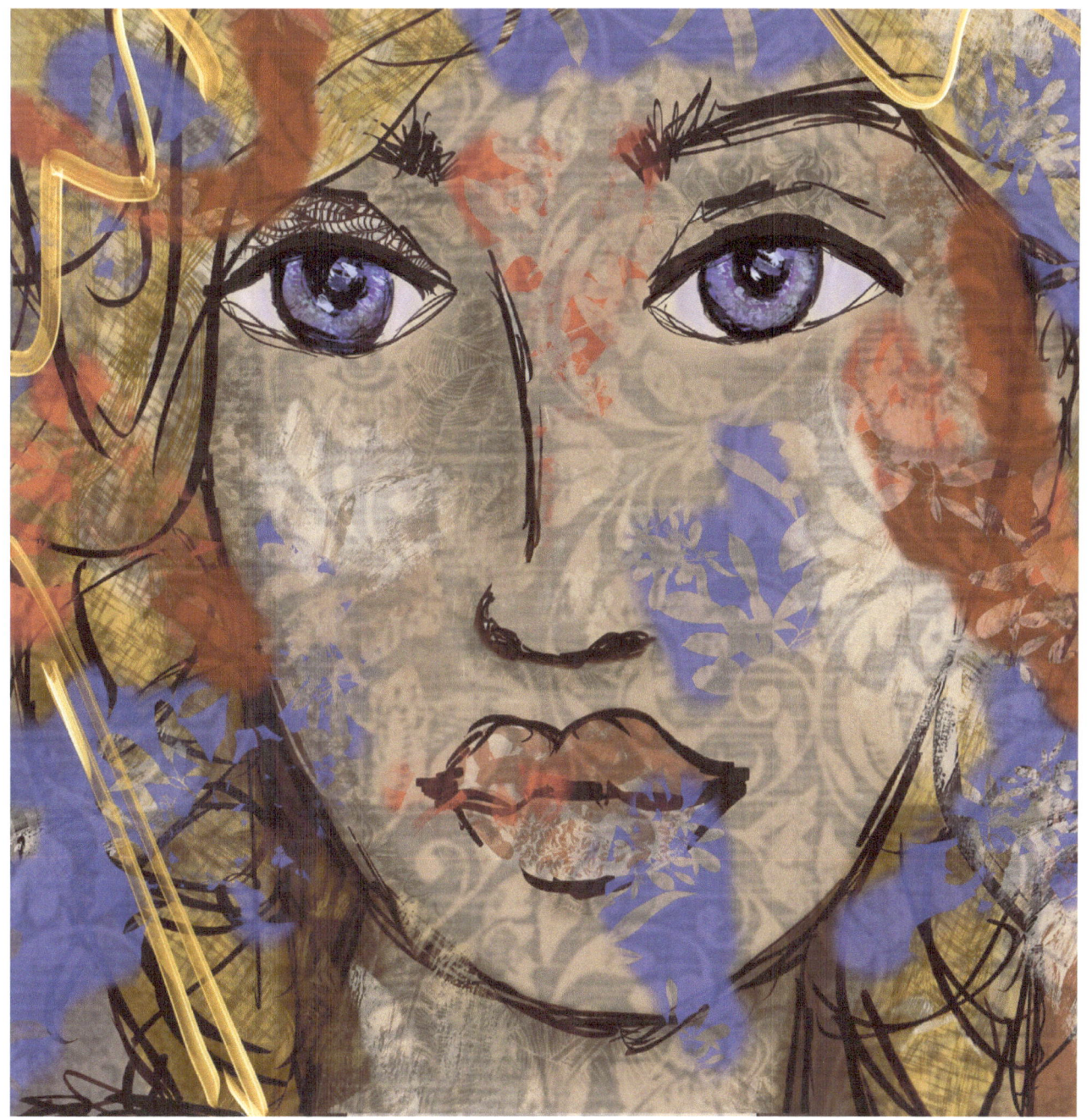

'Her Essence'   4173 x 4173 px

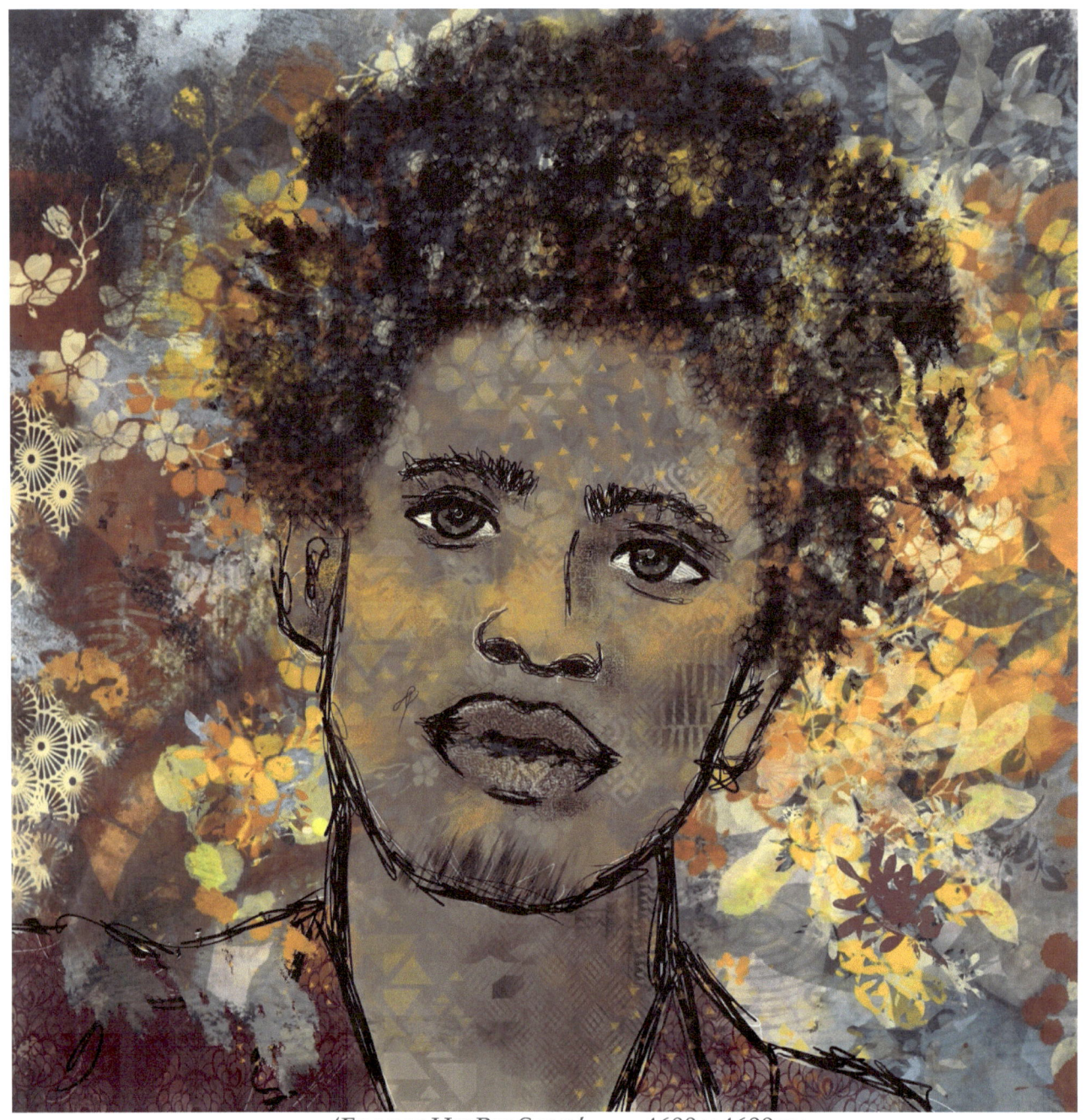

'FILLING HIS BIG SOUL'   4600 x 4600 px

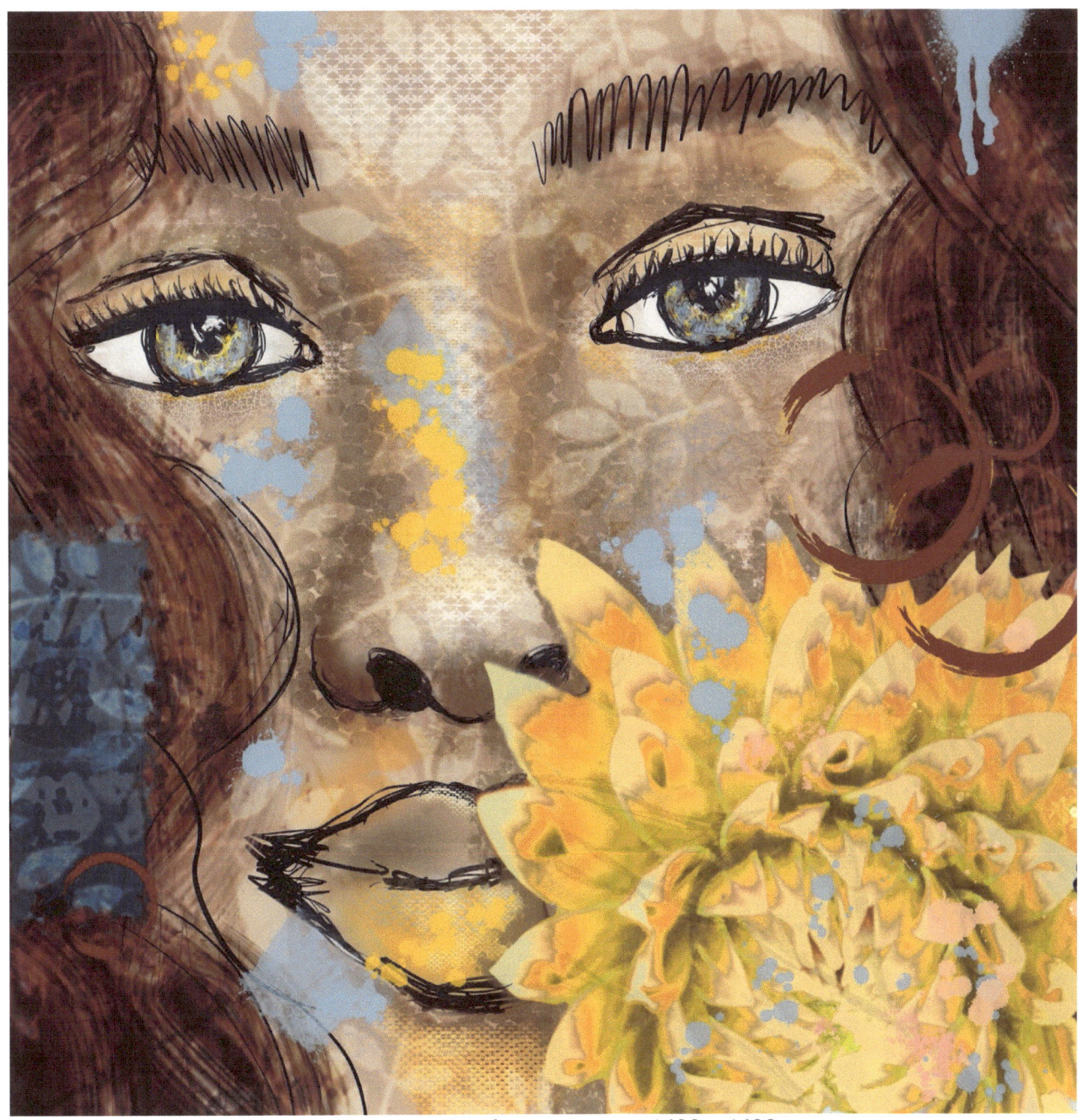

'Flower Girl' 4600 x 4600 px

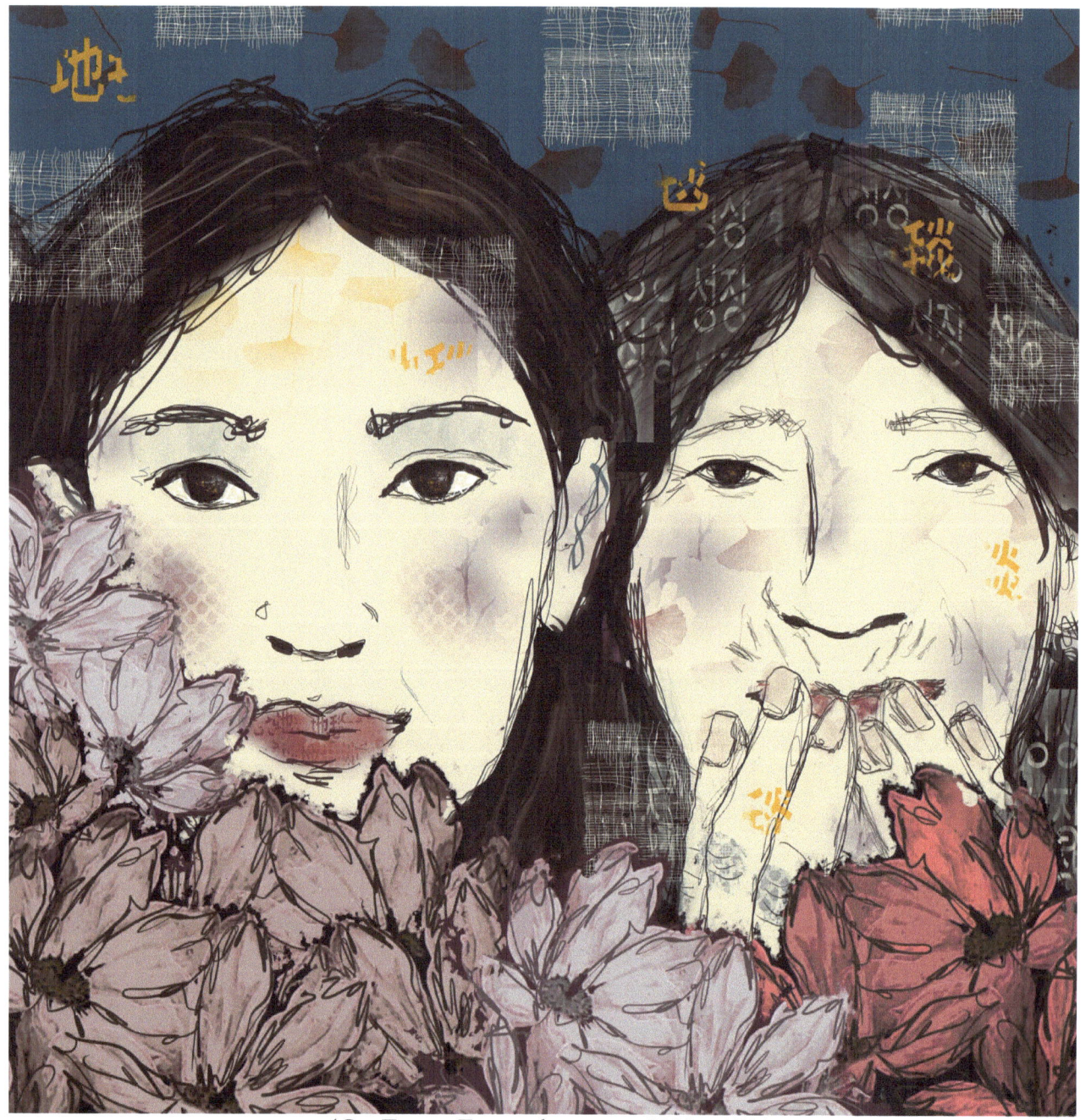

'Oh Those Elders' 4500 x 4500 px

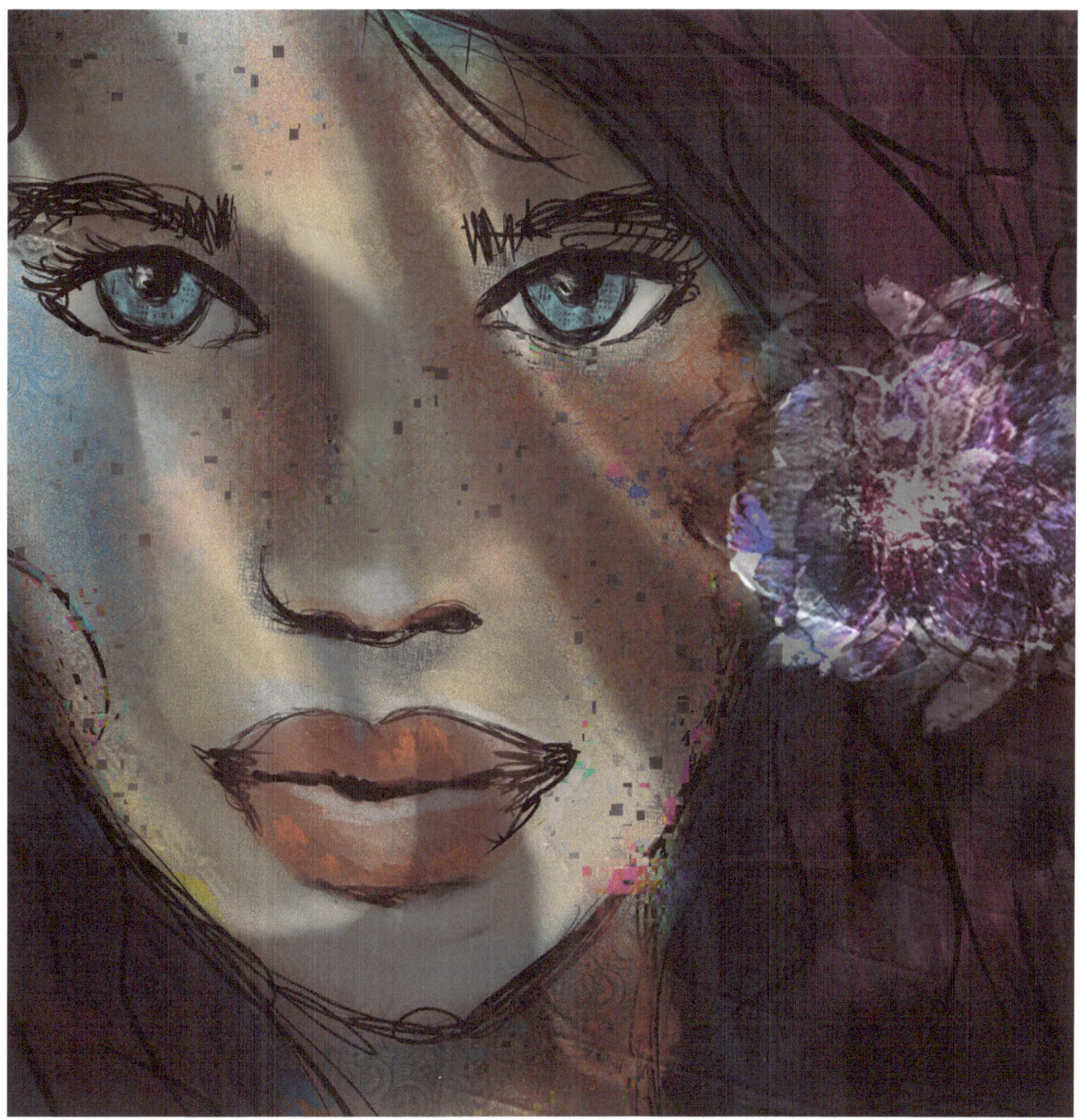

'Enchanting'   4600 x 4600 px

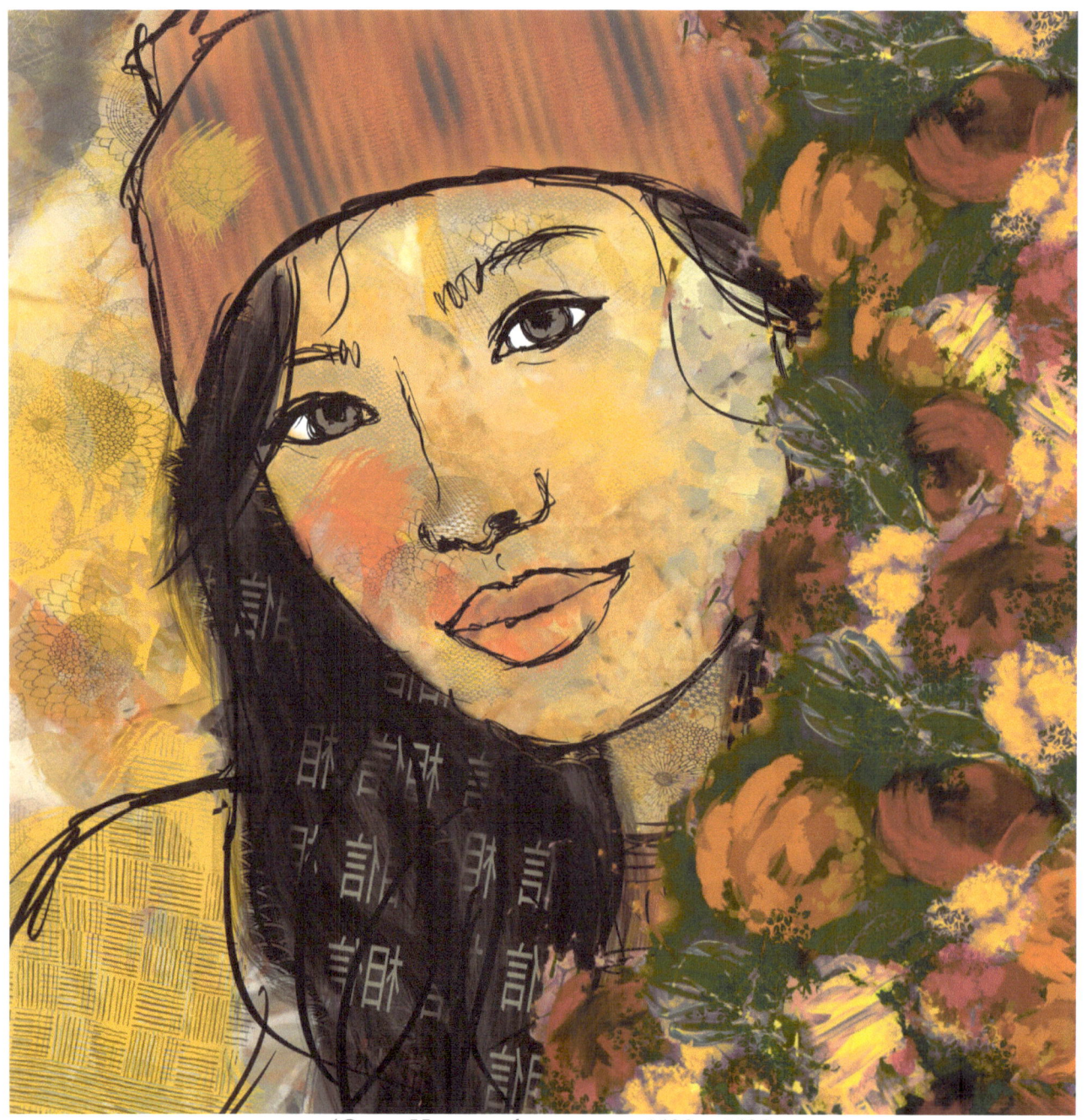

'Open-Hearted'   4600 x 4600 px

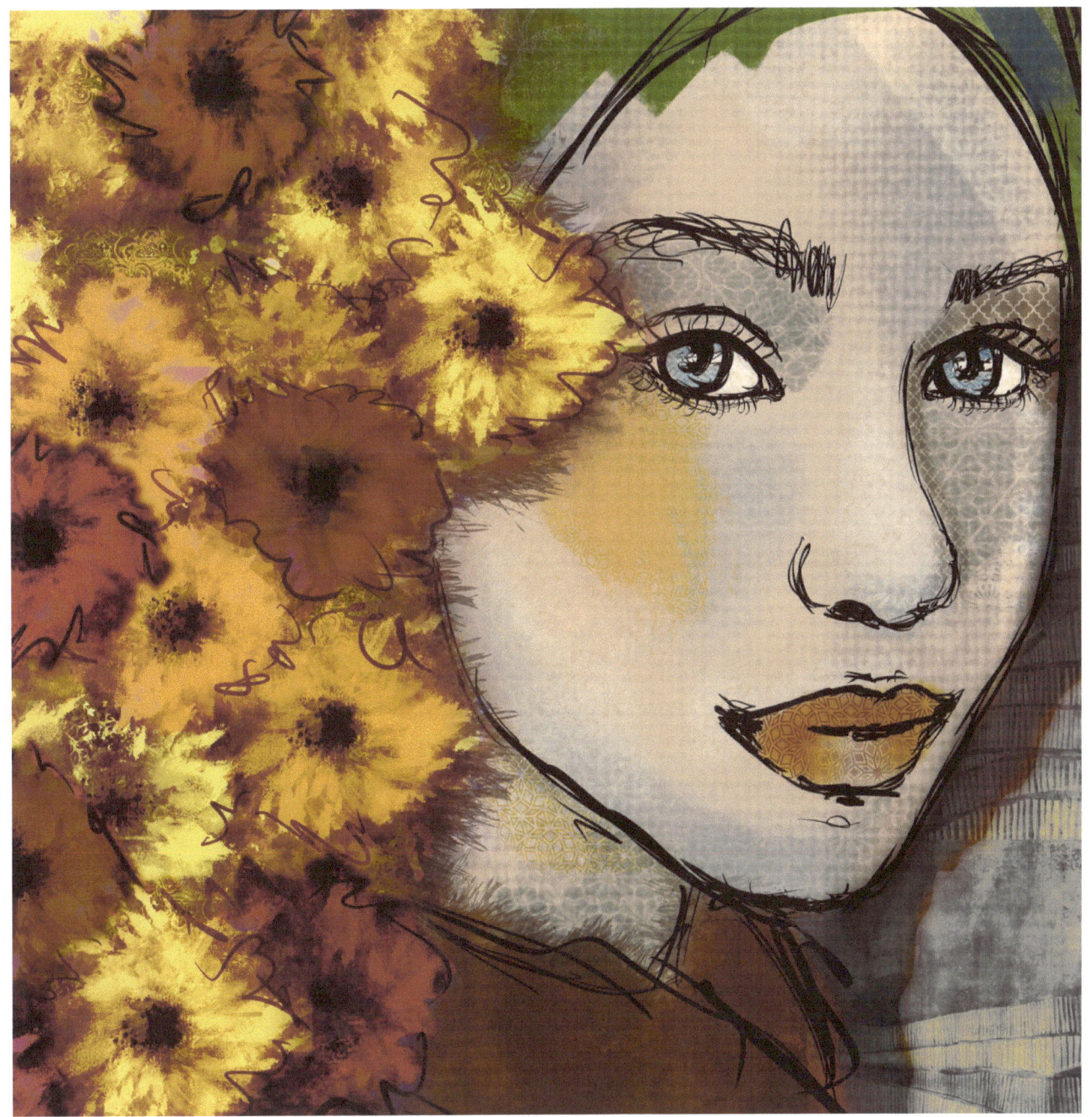

'Evening Shadows' 4600 x 4600 px

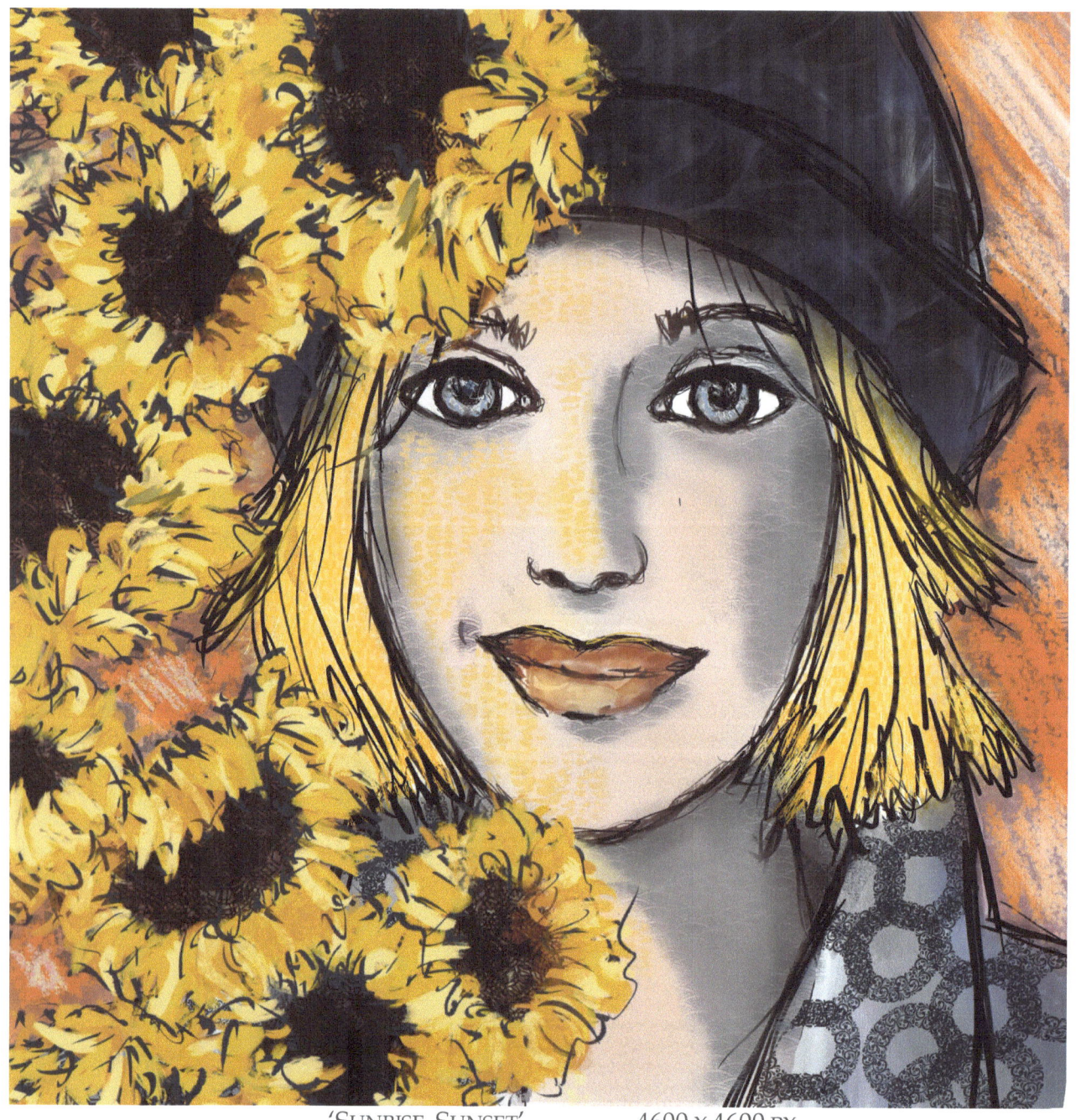

'Sunrise, Sunset' 4600 x 4600 px